SAXON MATH™
Intermediate 3

Standards Success
Common Core State Standards Companion
for use with *Saxon Math Intermediate 3*

SAXON®

HOUGHTON MIFFLIN HARCOURT

Table of Contents

Instructions for Using This Book

Educators who use Saxon Math know that the programs help students become competent and confident learners. Because of the incremental nature of the program, some lessons provide foundational instruction necessary for developing more advanced skills used in later lessons. The Power Up, Problem Solving, and Written Practice sections of each lesson provide important review and practice needed for mastery. For those reasons, it is essential to teach all the lessons in the correct order and to include all parts of the lesson in the daily instruction.

The program Table of Contents included in this book shows references to the primary Common Core State Standards domain and cluster or Mathematical Practice addressed by each lesson and investigation. The Lesson Extension Activities provided in this book will help reinforce that knowledge. Each of these activities was developed to spring from the instruction of the designated lesson or investigation.

It is recommended that you review the Table of Contents to understand where the extension lessons are to be integrated into the program. Then place a reminder in the Teacher's Manual, such as a colored flag or sticker, on the lesson or investigation with which the extension should be presented. Before the day the extension is to be taught, photocopy both the Lesson Extension Activity and Activity Master (one copy of each per student). The pages are perforated to make removal and copying easier. At this time, also check the extension activity and activity master for any materials that are required and be prepared for each student to have the necessary items. The problems on the Activity Masters may be solved directly following the Lesson Extension Activity, or may be used as additional practice at a later time.

Extension Tests are provided to ensure that all Common Core objectives are evaluated. These multiple-choice assessments should be given with specified Cumulative Tests, as noted in the Table of Contents. Before test day, photocopy one copy of the Extension Test for each student's use.

Best wishes for a successful school year!

Saxon Math Intermediate 3 Standards Success Overview

Common Core State Standards and the Saxon Math Pedagogy

The Saxon Math philosophy stresses that incremental and integrated instruction, with the opportunity to practice and internalize concepts, leads to successful mathematics understanding. This pedagogy aligns with the requirements of the Common Core State Standards, which emphasize that, in each grade, students will be instructed to mastery in specified math concepts that serve as a basis for future learning. For example, in Grade 3 students develop fluency in multiplication and division, as well as a greater understanding of fractions, that can be carried forward to succeeding grades. Having established this solid foundation, the students will have the necessary tools (speed, accuracy, and confidence in their ability) to tackle increasingly complex problem solving.

The requisites featured in the Mathematical Practices are incorporated throughout the Saxon lessons and activities. For example, students are asked to share ideas and to think critically, to look for patterns, and to make connections in mathematical reasoning.

What *Saxon Math Intermediate 3 Standards Success* Provides

Saxon Math Intermediate 3 Standards Success is a companion to *Saxon Math Intermediate 3*. The first section, the Table of Contents, lists the Common Core focus of each lesson. The second section, Correlation of *Saxon Math Intermediate 3* to the Common Core State Standards for Mathematics Grade 3, demonstrates the depth of coverage provided by the *Saxon Math Intermediate 3* program. The remaining sections, Lesson Extension Activities and Extension Tests, provide additional reinforcement for selected Common Core standards.

Saxon Math Intermediate 3 Table of Contents

The Intermediate 3 Table of Contents lists the primary Common Core domain and cluster addressed in the New Concept of each lesson and that section's Investigation. Some lessons focus on a Mathematical Practice, such as a problem-solving technique. The primary Common Core State Standards focuses in the Power Up and Problem Solving activities of the ten lessons are listed on a chart at the bottom of each page of the Table of Contents.

Correlation of *Saxon Math Intermediate 3* to the Common Core State Standards for Mathematics Grade 3

The correlation lists the specific *Saxon Math Intermediate 3* components addressing each standard. This correlation is divided into three sections: Power Up (including Power Up and Problem Solving), Lessons (including New Concepts, Investigations, and Written Practices), and Other (including Calculator Activities, Performance Tasks, and Test Day Activities).

Lesson Extension Activities and *Extension Tests*

Lesson Extension Activities (with Activity Masters on the back) and Extension Tests are listed in the Table of Contents where they are intended to be used. These additional activities further address and reinforce the Common Core standards. Lesson Extension Activities, Activity Masters, and Extension Tests begin on page 19 of this book.

Domains, Clusters, and Mathematical Practices for Grade 3

The Common Core State Standards are separated into domains, which are divided into clusters.

Grade 3 Domains and Clusters

Large groups of connected standards are referred to as domains. In Grade 3 there are five domains. Groups of related standards within a domain are referred to as clusters.

3.OA–Operations and Algebraic Thinking

1st cluster:	Represent and solve problems involving multiplication and division.
2nd cluster:	Understand properties of multiplication and the relationship between multiplication and division.
3rd cluster:	Multiply and divide within 100.
4th cluster:	Solve problems involving the four operations, and identify and explain patterns in arithmetic.

3.NBT–Number and Operations in Base Ten

1st cluster:	Use place value understanding and properties of operations to perform multi-digit arithmetic.

3.NF–Number and Operations—Fractions

1st cluster:	Develop understanding of fractions as numbers.

3.MD–Measurement and Data

1st cluster:	Solve problems involving measurement and estimation of intervals of time, liquid volumes, and masses of objects.
2nd cluster:	Represent and interpret data.
3rd cluster:	Geometric measurement: understand concepts of area and relate area to multiplication and to addition.
4th cluster:	Geometric measurement: recognize perimeter as an attribute of plane figures and distinguish between linear and area measures.

3.G–Geometry

1st cluster:	Reason with shapes and their attributes.

Mathematical Practices

The Standards for Mathematical Practice list the following essential competencies that students will develop throughout their mathematics education.

CC.K–12.MP.1	Make sense of problems and persevere in solving them.
CC.K–12.MP.2	Reason abstractly and quantitatively.
CC.K–12.MP.3	Construct viable arguments and critique the reasoning of others.
CC.K–12.MP.4	Model with mathematics.
CC.K–12.MP.5	Use appropriate tools strategically.
CC.K–12.MP.6	Attend to precision.
CC.K–12.MP.7	Look for and make use of structure.
CC.K–12.MP.8	Look for and express regularity in repeated reasoning.

For the full text of the Common Core State Standards and a comprehensive correlation, including Mathematical Practices, see the Correlation of *Saxon Math Intermediate 3* to the Common Core State Standards for Mathematics Grade 3 on pages 13–18.

 Saxon Math Intermediate 3

SAXON **MATH**™ Intermediate 3
TABLE OF CONTENTS

Common Core

Section 1 • Lessons 1–10, Investigation 1

The following table shows a CCSS (Common Core State Standards) focus of the Power Up (PU) and the Problem Solving (PS) activities, which appear at the beginning of each lesson.

CCSS Reference	1	2	3	4	5	6	7	8	9	10
CC.K–12.MP.1	PS	PS	PS	PS	PS	PS	PS	PS	PS	PS
CC.K–12.MP.4				PS						
CC.3.OA (4th cluster)		PU								
CC.3.MD (1st cluster)	PU	PU	PU	PU	PU	PU	PU	PU	PU	PU

Correlation references are read as follows: CC indicates Common Core, the number following is the grade, the letters indicate the domain, and the cluster indicates the particular group of related standards. Mathematical Practices are described in the same way for all grades K–12.

MP Mathematical Practices   **OA** Operations and Algebraic Thinking   **NBT** Number and Operations in Base Ten
NF Number and Operations—Fractions   **MD** Measurement and Data   **G** Geometry

Lesson		CCSS Focus of Lesson
11	• Place Value	CC.K–12.MP.7
12	• Reading and Writing Numbers Through 999	CC.K–12.MP.7
13	• Adding Two-Digit Numbers	CC.3.NBT (1st cluster)
14	• Subtracting Two-Digit Numbers	CC.3.NBT (1st cluster)
15	• Rounding to the Nearest Ten and Hundred	CC.3.NBT (1st cluster)
	Cumulative Assessment	
16	• Adding Three-Digit Numbers	CC.3.NBT (1st cluster)
17	• Comparing and Ordering, Part 1	CC.K–12.MP.5
18	• Some and Some More Stories, Part 1	CC.3.OA (4th cluster)
19	• Subtracting Three-Digit Numbers, Part 1	CC.3.NBT (1st cluster)
20	• Some Went Away Stories, Part 1	CC.3.OA (4th cluster)
Inv. 2	• Working with Money	CC.3.NBT (1st cluster)
	Cumulative Assessment	

The following table shows a CCSS focus of the Power Up (PU) and the Problem Solving (PS) activities, which appear at the beginning of each lesson.

CCSS Reference	11	12	13	14	15	16	17	18	19	20
CC.K–12.MP.1	PS	PS	PS	PS	PS	PS	PS	PS	PS	PS
CC.K–12.MP.2		PS						PS		PS
CC.K–12.MP.4							PS			
CC.K–12.MP.6										PS
CC.K–12.MP.7	PS									
CC.3.OA (4th cluster)			PU							
CC.3.NBT (1st cluster)	PU	PU	PU	PU	PU	PU	PU	PU	PU	PU
CC.3.MD (1st cluster)	PU	PU	PU	PU	PU	PU	PU	PU	PU	PU

Lesson		CCSS Focus of Lesson
21	• Naming Dollars and Cents • Exchanging Dollars, Dimes, and Pennies	CC.K–12.MP.4
22	• Adding Dollars and Cents	CC.K–12.MP.5
23	• Subtracting Three-Digit Numbers, Part 2	CC.3.NBT (1st cluster)
24	• Column Addition	CC.3.NBT (1st cluster)
25	• Counting Dollars and Cents	CC.K–12.MP.4
	Cumulative Assessment	
26	• Subtracting Dollars and Cents	CC.K–12.MP.5
27	• Comparing and Ordering, Part 2	CC.K–12.MP.7
28	• Subtracting Across Zeros	CC.3.NBT (1st cluster)
29	• Fractions of a Dollar	CC.3.NF (1st cluster)
30	• Estimating Sums and Differences	CC.3.NBT (1st cluster)
Inv. 3	• More About Pictographs	CC.3.MD (2nd cluster)
	Cumulative Assessment	

The following table shows a CCSS focus of the Power Up (PU) and the Problem Solving (PS) activities, which appear at the beginning of each lesson.

CCSS Reference	21	22	23	24	25	26	27	28	29	30
CC.K–12.MP.1	PS	PS	PS	PS	PS	PS	PS	PS	PS	PS
CC.K–12.MP.4								PS		
CC.K–12.MP.7				PS						
CC.3.OA (4th cluster)			PU	PS						
CC.3.NBT (1st cluster)	PU								PU	
CC.3.MD (1st cluster)	PU	PU	PU	PU	PU	PU	PU	PU	PU	PU

MP Mathematical Practices   **OA** Operations and Algebraic Thinking   **NBT** Number and Operations in Base Ten
NF Number and Operations—Fractions   **MD** Measurement and Data   **G** Geometry

Lesson		CCSS Focus of Lesson
31	• Writing Directions	CC.K–12.MP.6
32	• Reading and Writing Numbers Through 999,999	CC.K–12.MP.7
33	• More About Number Lines	CC.K–12.MP.4
34	• Length: Inches, Feet, and Yards	CC.3.MD (2nd cluster)
35	• Measuring to the Nearest Quarter Inch Lesson Extension Activity 1 (p 19): • Making a Line Plot to Show Measurement Data	CC.3.MD (2nd cluster)
	Cumulative Assessment	
36	• Some and Some More Stories, Part 2	CC.3.OA (4th cluster)
37	• Estimating Lengths and Distances	CC.3.MD (2nd cluster)
38	• Reading a Clock to the Nearest Minute Lesson Extension Activity 2 (p 21): • Measuring Time Intervals	CC.3.MD (1st cluster)
39	• Stories About Comparing	CC.3.OA (4th cluster)
40	• Missing Numbers in Subtraction • Some Went Away Stories, Part 2	CC.3.OA (4th cluster)
Inv. 4	• Scale Maps	CC.K–12.MP.5
	Cumulative Assessment	

The following table shows a CCSS focus of the Power Up (PU) and the Problem Solving (PS) activities, which appear at the beginning of each lesson.

CCSS Reference	31	32	33	34	35	36	37	38	39	40
CC.K–12.MP.1	PS	PS	PS	PS	PS	PS	PS	PS	PS	PS
CC.3.OA (4th cluster)			PU			PU	PU		PU	
CC.3.NBT (1st cluster)	PU	PU	PU	PU						
CC.3.MD (1st cluster)		PU	PU	PU		PU	PU		PU	PU

Saxon Math Intermediate 3

Lesson		CCSS Focus of Lesson
41	• Modeling Fractions	CC.3.NF (1st cluster)
42	• Drawing Fractions	CC.3.NF (1st cluster)
43	• Comparing Fractions, Part 1	CC.3.NF (1st cluster)
44	• Fractions of a Group	CC.K–12.MP.3
45	• Probability, Part 1	CC.K–12.MP.3
	Cumulative Assessment *Extension Test 1*	
46	• Fractions Equal to 1 • Mixed Numbers	CC.3.NF (1st cluster)
47	• Equivalent Fractions	CC.3.NF (1st cluster)
48	• Finding Fractions and Mixed Numbers on a Number Line	CC.3.NF (1st cluster)
49	• Comparing Fractions, Part 2	CC.3.NF (1st cluster)
50	• Probability, Part 2	CC.K–12.MP.3
Inv. 5	• Probability Games	CC.K–12.MP.3
	Cumulative Assessment	

The following table shows a CCSS focus of the Power Up (PU) and the Problem Solving (PS) activities, which appear at the beginning of each lesson.

CCSS Reference	41	42	43	44	45	46	47	48	49	50
CC.K–12.MP.1	PS	PS	PS	PS	PS	PS	PS	PS	PS	PS
CC.K–12.MP.2										PS
CC.K–12.MP.3	PS								PS	
CC.K–12.MP.4							PS			
CC.K–12.MP.7						PS				
CC.K–12.MP.8							PS			
CC.3.OA (4th cluster)							PU			
CC.3.NBT (1st cluster)							PU			
CC.3.MD (1st cluster)	PU	PU	PU	PU	PU	PU	PU		PU	PU

MP Mathematical Practices   **OA** Operations and Algebraic Thinking   **NBT** Number and Operations in Base Ten
NF Number and Operations—Fractions   **MD** Measurement and Data   **G** Geometry

Lesson		CCSS Focus of Lesson
51	• Rectangles	CC.3.G (1st cluster)
52	• Length and Width	CC.3.MD (2nd cluster)
53	• Rectangular Grid Patterns	CC.3.MD (3rd cluster)
54	• Multiplication as Repeated Addition	CC.3.OA (1st cluster)
55	• Multiplication Table	CC.3.OA (2nd cluster)
	Cumulative Assessment	
	Extension Test 2	
56	• Multiplication Facts: 0s, 1s, and 10s	CC.3.OA (2nd cluster)
57	• Arrays	CC.3.OA (1st cluster)
58	• Perimeter	CC.3.MD (4th cluster)
59	• Multiplication Facts: 2s and 5s	CC.3.OA (3rd cluster)
60	• Equal Groups Stories, Part 1	CC.3.OA (1st cluster)
Inv. 6	• More About Bar Graphs	CC.3.MD (2nd cluster)
	Cumulative Assessment	

The following table shows a CCSS focus of the Power Up (PU) and the Problem Solving (PS) activities, which appear at the beginning of each lesson.

CCSS Reference	51	52	53	54	55	56	57	58	59	60
CC.K–12.MP.1	PS	PS	PS	PS	PS	PS	PS	PS	PS	PS
CC.K–12.MP.2										PS
CC.K–12.MP.3					PS					
CC.K–12.MP.4	PS									
CC.K–12.MP.7	PS					PS		PS		
CC.3.OA (1st cluster)					PS					
CC.3.OA (3rd cluster)							PU	PU	PU	PU
CC.3.OA (4th cluster)	PU				PS					PU
CC.3.NBT (1st cluster)			PU					PU	PU	
CC.3.NF (1st cluster)		PU	PU		PU				PU	
CC.3.MD (1st cluster)	PU		PU	PU	PU	PU		PU		
CC.3.MD (3rd cluster)				PS						

Saxon Math Intermediate 3

Lesson		CCSS Focus of Lesson
61	• Squares • Multiplication Facts: Square Numbers	CC.3.OA (4th cluster)
62	• Area, Part 1 Lesson Extension Activity 3 (p 23): • Rectangles with the Same Area or Same Perimeter	CC.3.MD (3rd cluster) CC.3.MD (4th cluster)
63	• Area, Part 2 Lesson Extension Activity 4 (p 25): • Relating Shapes, Fractions, and Area	CC.3.MD (3rd cluster) CC.3.G (1st cluster)
64	• Multiplication Facts: 9s	CC.3.OA (3rd cluster)
65	• Angles	CC.K–12.MP.6
	Cumulative Assessment *Extension Test 3*	
66	• Parallelograms	CC.3.G (1st cluster)
67	• Polygons Lesson Extension Activity 5 (p 27): • Finding an Unknown Side Length	CC.3.G (1st cluster) CC.3.MD (4th cluster)
68	• Congruent Shapes	CC.K–12.MP.3
69	• Triangles	CC.3.G (1st cluster)
70	• Multiplication Facts: Memory Group	CC.3.OA (3rd cluster)
Inv. 7	• Symmetry, Part 1	CC.K–12.MP.5
	Cumulative Assessment *Extension Test 4*	

The following table shows a CCSS focus of the Power Up (PU) and the Problem Solving (PS) activities, which appear at the beginning of each lesson.

CCSS Reference	61	62	63	64	65	66	67	68	69	70
CC.K–12.MP.1	PS	PS	PS	PS	PS	PS	PS	PS	PS	PS
CC.K–12.MP.2				PS						
CC.K–12.MP.6									PS	
CC.3.OA (1st cluster)		PS	PU			PU		PU		
CC.3.OA (3rd cluster)	PU	PU	PU	PU	PU	PU	PU		PU	PU
CC.3.OA (4th cluster)	PU			PU	PS					
CC.3.NBT (1st cluster)			PU							PU
CC.3.NF (1st cluster)		PU	PU					PU		
CC.3.MD (1st cluster)	PU	PU		PU					PS	
CC.3.MD (4th cluster)							PU		PU	
CC.3.G (1st cluster)	PU		PU					PU		PU

MP Mathematical Practices **OA** Operations and Algebraic Thinking **NBT** Number and Operations in Base Ten
NF Number and Operations—Fractions **MD** Measurement and Data **G** Geometry

Section 8 • Lessons 71–80, Investigation 8

Lesson		CCSS Focus of Lesson
71	• Rectangular Prisms	CC.K–12.MP.3
72	• Counting Cubes	CC.K–12.MP.7
73	• Volume	CC.K–12.MP.7
74	• Weight: Ounces, Pounds, and Tons	CC.3.MD (1st cluster)
75	• Geometric Solids	CC.K–12.MP.3
	Cumulative Assessment *Extension Test 5*	
76	• Multiplication Facts: 11s and 12s	CC.3.OA (4th cluster)
77	• Multiplying Three Numbers	CC.3.OA (3rd cluster)
78	• Multiplying Multiples of Ten	CC.3.NBT (1st cluster)
79	• Length: Centimeters, Meters, and Kilometers	CC.3.MD (3rd cluster)
80	• Mass: Grams and Kilograms	CC.3.MD (3rd cluster)
Inv. 8	• More About Geometric Solids	CC.K–12.MP.3
	Cumulative Assessment	

The following table shows a CCSS focus of the Power Up (PU) and the Problem Solving (PS) activities, which appear at the beginning of each lesson.

CCSS Reference	71	72	73	74	75	76	77	78	79	80
CC.K–12.MP.1	PS	PS	PS	PS	PS	PS	PS	PS	PS	PS
CC.K–12.MP.2								PS		
CC.K–12.MP.3							PS			
CC.3.OA (1st cluster)			PU	PU	PS	PU		PU		PU
CC.3.OA (3rd cluster)		PU	PU	PU	PU	PU	PU	PU	PU	PU
CC.3.OA (4th cluster)		PU		PU		PU				
CC.3.NBT (1st cluster)					PU				PU	
CC.3.NF (1st cluster)	PU				PU	PU				
CC.3.MD (1st cluster)	PU/PS	PU				PU	PU	PU		
CC.3.MD (4th cluster)			PU					PU		
CC.3.G (1st cluster)		PU	PU		PU/PS	PU			PU	

Saxon Math Intermediate 3

Section 9 • Lessons 81–90, Investigation 9

Lesson		CCSS Focus of Lesson
81	• Multiplying Two-Digit Numbers, Part 1	CC.3.OA (3rd cluster)
82	• Fair Share	CC.3.OA (1st cluster)
83	• Finding Half of a Number	CC.3.OA (3rd cluster)
84	• Multiplying Two-Digit Numbers, Part 2	CC.3.OA (3rd cluster)
	Lesson Extension Activity 6 (p 29):	
	• Finding Area of Combined Rectangles	CC.3.MD (3rd cluster)
85	• Using Manipulatives to Divide by a One-Digit Number	CC.3.OA (1st cluster)
	Cumulative Assessment	
86	• Division Facts	CC.3.OA (3rd cluster)
	• Multiplication and Division Fact Families	
87	• Capacity	
	Lesson Extension Activity 7 (p 31):	CC.3.MD (1st cluster)
	• Estimating and Measuring Liquid Volume	
88	• Even and Odd Numbers	CC.3.OA (4th cluster)
89	• Using a Multiplication Table to Divide by a One-Digit Number	CC.3.OA (3rd cluster)
90	• Equal Groups Stories, Part 2	CC.3.OA (1st cluster)
Inv. 9	• Symmetry, Part 2	CC.K–12.MP.5
	Cumulative Assessment	
	Extension Test 6	

CCSS Reference	81	82	83	84	85	86	87	88	89	90
CC.K–12.MP.1	PS	PS	PS	PS	PS	PS	PS	PS	PS	PS
CC.K–12.MP.2		PS								
CC.K–12.MP.3				PS						
CC.K–12.MP.6							PS			
CC.K–12.MP.7						PS				
CC.K–12.MP.8								PU		PU
CC.3.OA (1st cluster)		PS	PU	PU		PU	PU		PU	PU/PS
CC.3.OA (2nd cluster)						PU				
CC.3.OA (3rd cluster)	PU	PU	PU	PU		PU	PU	PU	PU	PU
CC.3.OA (4th cluster)						PS	PS			PU
CC.3.NBT (1st cluster)	PU	PU			PU		PU	PU		PU
CC.3.NF (1st cluster)			PU			PU				
CC.3.MD (1st cluster)					PU		PS		PU	PU
CC.3.MD (3rd cluster)		PS								
CC.3.MD (4th cluster)				PU				PU		
CC.3.G (1st cluster)		PU	PU	PU			PU	PU		PU

MP Mathematical Practices   **OA** Operations and Algebraic Thinking   **NBT** Number and Operations in Base Ten
NF Number and Operations—Fractions   **MD** Measurement and Data   **G** Geometry

Lesson		CCSS Focus of Lesson
91	• Multiplying Three-Digit Numbers, Part 1	CC.K–12.MP.2
92	• Parentheses • Using Compatible Numbers, Part 1 Lesson Extension Activity 8 (p 33): • Using Order of Operations	CC.3.OA (3rd cluster) CC.K–12.MP.4 CC.3.OA (4th cluster)
93	• Estimating Products	CC.3.NBT (1st cluster)
94	• Using Compatible Numbers, Part 2	CC.K–12.MP.4
95	• Using Estimation to Verify Answers Lesson Extension Activity 9 (p 35): • Solving Two-Step Word Problems	CC.3.NBT (1st cluster) CC.3.OA (4th cluster)
	Cumulative Assessment *Extension Test 7*	
96	• Rounding to the Nearest Dollar	CC.K–12.MP.4
97	• Multiplying Three-Digit Numbers, Part 2	CC.K–12.MP.1
98	• Estimating by Weight or Mass	CC.3.MD (1st cluster)
99	• Effects of Estimation	CC.3.OA (1st cluster)
100	• Multiplying Dollars and Cents	CC.3.OA (1st cluster)
Inv. 10	• Evaluating Estimates	CC.K–12.MP.3
	Cumulative Assessment *Extension Test 8*	

The following table shows a CCSS focus of the Power Up (PU) and the Problem Solving (PS) activities, which appear at the beginning of each lesson.

CCSS Reference	91	92	93	94	95	96	97	98	99	100
CC.K–12.MP.1	PS	PS	PS	PS	PS	PS	PS	PS	PS	PS
CC.K–12.MP.3										PS
CC.K–12.MP.7					PS					
CC.K–12.MP.8							PS			
CC.3.OA (1st cluster)	PU	PU	PU/PS	PS			PU			PU
CC.3.OA (2nd cluster)	PU	PU	PU			PU	PU			
CC.3.OA (3rd cluster)	PU	PU	PU	PU	PU	PU	PU	PU	PU	PU
CC.3.NBT (1st cluster)	PU		PU	PU	PU	PU			PU	PU
CC.3.NF (1st cluster)				PU	PU					PU
CC.3.MD (1st cluster)		PU		PU					PU	
CC.3.MD (3rd cluster)			PU							
CC.3.MD (4th cluster)			PU					PU		
CC.3.G (1st cluster)				PU	PU			PU		PU/PS

Section 11 • Lessons 101–110, Investigation 11

Lesson		CCSS Focus of Lesson
101	• Dividing Two-Digit Numbers	CC.3.OA (1st cluster)
102	• Sorting	CC.K–12.MP.7
103	• Ordering Numbers Through 9,999	CC.K–12.MP.7
104	• Sorting Geometric Shapes Lesson Extension Activity 10 (p 37): • Classifying Quadrilaterals	CC.3.G (1st cluster)
105	• Diagrams for Sorting	CC.3.G (1st cluster)
	Cumulative Assessment *Extension Test 9*	
106	• Estimating Area, Part 1	CC.3.MD (3rd cluster)
107	• Drawing Enlargements	CC.K–12.MP.6
108	• Estimating Area, Part 2	CC.3.MD (3rd cluster)
109	• Points on a Grid	CC.K–12.MP.6
110	• Dot-to-Dot Design	CC.K–12.MP.6
Inv. 11	• Planning a Design	CC.K–12.MP.6
	Cumulative Assessment *Extension Test 10*	

The following table shows a CCSS focus of the Power Up (PU) and the Problem Solving (PS) activities, which appear at the beginning of each lesson.

CCSS Reference	101	102	103	104	105	106	107	108	109	110
CC.K–12.MP.1	PS	PS	PS	PS	PS	PS	PS	PS	PS	PS
CC.K–12.MP.2							PS			
CC.K–12.MP.6										PS
CC.K–12.MP.7		PS								
CC.K–12.MP.8					PS					
CC.3.OA (1st cluster)	PU				PU/PS					
CC.3.OA (2nd cluster)	PU			PU	PU			PU		PU
CC.3.OA (3rd cluster)	PU	PU	PU	PU	PU	PU	PU	PU	PU	PU
CC.3.OA (4th cluster)	PS	PU	PU/PS	PU		PU	PS	PU/PS	PU	PU
CC.3.NBT (1st cluster)				PU			PU			
CC.3.MD (1st cluster)		PU	PU				PU			
CC.3.MD (3rd cluster)			PU					PU		
CC.3.G (1st cluster)				PU			PU			

MP Mathematical Practices **OA** Operations and Algebraic Thinking **NBT** Number and Operations in Base Ten
NF Number and Operations—Fractions **MD** Measurement and Data **G** Geometry

Correlation of *Saxon Math Intermediate 3* to the Common Core State Standards for Mathematics Grade 3

Mathematical Practices – *These standards are covered throughout the program; the following are examples.*

1. Make sense of problems and persevere in solving them.	**Power Up:** PS23, PS53, PS78, PS85, PS94, PS98, PS108 **Lessons:** Problem Solving Overview pp 1–6, L18, L20, WP22, L30, WP32, L36, L39, L40, WP41, WP50, L60, WP67, WP85, L90, L93, L95, L99, Inv10, WP106, WP109
2. Reason abstractly and quantitatively.	**Power Up:** PS12, PS18, PS20, PS50, PS60, PS64, PS78, PS82, PS107 **Lessons:** L9, L18, L20, L25, WP29, L34, L36, WP36, L39, L40, WP44, L58, WP59, L60, WP60, L62, L63, WP65, WP69, L72, L73, WP84, L90, WP94 **Other:** PT3, PT8
3. Construct viable arguments and critique the reasoning of others.	**Power Up:** PS41, PS49, PS55, PS77, PS84, PS100 **Lessons:** L26, L27, WP42, L44, L51, WP58, WP61, L67, L68, Inv8, WP95, L102, L104 **Other:** PT9
4. Model with mathematics.	**Power Up:** PS7, PS17, PS28, PS47, PS51 **Lessons:** L6, L7, Inv1, L11, L13, L14, L16, Inv2, WP21, Inv3, L34, WP38, WP39, WP40, WP42, WP46, WP60, Inv6, L81, WP91 **Other:** PT1, PT4, PT11
5. Use appropriate tools strategically.	**Lessons:** WP3, WP5, WP6, WP11, L14, L17, WP17, L19, L34, L35, L37, L38, WP38, Inv4, L65, L77, L79, L81, L85, WP85, WP86, Inv9, WP110 **Other:** CA16, CA19, CA60, CA73, PT10, CA101
6. Attend to precision.	**Power Up:** PS20, PS69, PS87, PS110 **Lessons:** L3, L4, L5, L20, WP22, WP31, L34, L35, L37, L38, Inv4, WP41, L52, L74, L79, L80, L84, WP84, WP86, L87, WP88, WP89, WP98, L109 **Other:** PT10
7. Look for and make use of structure.	**Power Up:** PS11, PS24, PS46, PS56, PS58, PS86, PS95, PS102 **Lessons:** L8, L10, WP10, L25, WP26, L34, L53, WP53, L77, L78, WP78, L92, WP93, L102, WP103, L104 **Other:** PT4, PT5
8. Look for and express regularity in repeated reasoning.	**Power Up:** PS47, PU88, PU90, PS97, PS105 **Lessons:** L15, WP26, L43, L44, L46, L47, WP47, L53, L54, L55, L56, L57, L58, L61, WP67, L70, L76, WP80, L81, L82, L83, L84, L86, WP86, L88, WP89, L101, L102, WP109 **Other:** PT7

Common Core State Standards	*Saxon Math Intermediate 3* *Italic references indicate foundational.*

Operations and Algebraic Thinking 3.OA

Represent and solve problems involving multiplication and division.

1. Interpret products of whole numbers, e.g., interpret 5 x 7 as the total number of objects in 5 groups of 7 objects each.	**Power Up:** PS55, PS62, PU63, PU66, PU68, PU73, PU74, PS75, PU76, PU78, PU80, PU84, PU86, PU89–PU91, PS94, PU97, PU100, PU101 **Lessons:** L54, WP54, L55, WP55, WP56, L57, WP57–WP59, L60, WP60, L61, WP61–WP64, WP66, WP67, WP70, WP73, WP75, WP76, WP78, WP79, WP81, WP84, WP102, WP104 **Other:** PUT9, LS54, LS57, LS59, LS60, BT3, LS61, CT12, CT13, CT15, CT19, BT5, CT20, ECE

Key:	**BT:** Benchmark Test	**ET:** Extension Test	**LXA:** Lesson Extension Activity	**PUT:** Power Up Test
	CA: Calculator Activity	**Inv:** Investigation	**PS:** Problem Solving	**TDA:** Test-Day Activity
	CT: Cumulative Test	**L:** Lesson	**PT:** Performance Task	**WP:** Written Practice
	ECE: End-of-Course Exam	**LS:** Learning Station	**PU:** Power Up	

2. Interpret whole-number quotients of whole numbers, e.g., interpret 56 ÷ 8 as the number of objects in each share when 56 objects are partitioned equally into 8 shares, or as a number of shares when 56 objects are partitioned into equal shares of 8 objects each.	**Power Up:** PU92, PU93, PS93, PS94 **Lessons:** L82, WP82–WP84, L85, WP85, L86, WP86, WP87, L88, WP88, WP89, L90, WP90, WP93, WP94, WP97, L101, WP105, WP108, WP109, WP110 **Other:** LS82, LS85, CT17, CT18, CT19, CT20, CT21, ECE
3. Use multiplication and division within 100 to solve word problems in situations involving equal groups, arrays, and measurement quantities, e.g., by using drawings and equations with a symbol for the unknown number to represent the problem.	**Power Up:** PS82, PU83, PS90, PS93, PS94, PS105 **Lessons:** L60, WP60–WP65, WP68–WP70, WP73, WP75, L76, WP76–WP78, L79, WP79, L80, L82, WP82, L83, L85, L87, L89, L90, WP90, WP91, WP93, WP94, L95, L97, L99, L100, WP100, WP101–WP104, WP107 **Other:** LS60, BT3, CT12, TDA6, PUT13, PT7, CT14, CT15, LS90, CT18, LS100, CT19, BT5, CT21, ECE
4. Determine the unknown whole number in a multiplication or division equation relating three whole numbers.	**Power Up:** PU87, PU92, PU101, PU105 **Lessons:** L86, WP86–WP88, L89, WP89, L90, WP91–WP107, WP109, WP110 **Other:** CT19, CT20, CT21, ECE

Understand properties of multiplication and the relationship between multiplication and division.

5. Apply properties of operations as strategies to multiply and divide.[1]	**Power Up:** PU86, PU91, PU92 **Lessons:** L55, WP55, L56, WP56, L57, WP57–WP59, WP62, WP64, L70, L77, WP77, WP78, WP80, L81, WP81–WP84, L86, WP87, WP88, L89, WP89, WP90, WP92, WP94, WP106, WP109, WP110 **Other:** BT4, CT16, CT17, CT18, CT19, CT21
6. Understand division as an unknown-factor problem.	**Power Up:** PU91–PU93, PU96, PU98, PU101, PU104, PU105, PU108, PU110 **Lessons:** L83, WP83–WP85, L86, WP86–WP88, L89, WP89, L90, WP90–WP94, WP105, WP107 **Other:** LS86, CT18, CT19, CT20, CT21

Multiply and divide within 100.

7. Fluently multiply and divide within 100, using strategies such as the relationship between multiplication and division (e.g., knowing that 8 x 5 = 40, one knows 40 ÷ 5 = 8) or properties of operations. By the end of Grade 3, know from memory all products of two one-digit numbers.	**Power Up:** PU57–PU67, PU69, PU70, PU72–PU84, PU86–PU110 **Lessons:** L54, L55, WP55, L56, WP56–WP58, L59, WP59, WP60, L61, WP61, WP63, L64, WP64, WP65, WP68, WP69, L70, WP70–WP76, L77, WP78–WP80, L81, WP81, L83, L86, WP86, WP87, L89, WP89, L92, WP101 **Other:** LS54–LS56, LS59, LS64, LS70, LS86, CT17, CT18, CT21

Solve problems involving the four operations, and identify and explain patterns in arithmetic.

8. Solve two-step word problems using the four operations. Represent these problems using equations with a letter standing for the unknown quantity. Assess the reasonableness of answers using mental computation and estimation strategies including rounding.[2]	**Power Up:** PU36, PU37, PU47, PU51, PU60, PU61, PU72, PU76, PU90, PU102, PU103, PS103, PU104, PU106, PS107, PU108, PS108, PU110 **Lessons:** WP2, WP7, WP8, L9, WP9, WP10, WP13, WP15, WP16, L18, WP18, WP19, L20, WP20–WP35, L36, WP37, WP38, L39, WP39, L40, WP40–WP55, WP57, WP59, L60, WP60–WP89, L90, WP90–WP110 **Other:** PT1, TDA6, LXA8, LXA9, ET8, ET9
9. Identify arithmetic patterns (including patterns in the addition table or multiplication table), and explain them using properties of operations.	**Power Up:** PU2, PU13, PU23, PS24, PU33, PU39, PS55, PU64, PS65, PU74, PS86, PS87, PS101, PU109 **Lessons:** L2, WP4–WP8, WP10–WP14, WP16–WP19, WP33, L34, L61, WP61, L64, WP64, WP65–WP67, WP69, WP71–WP73, WP75, L76, WP76, WP78, L88, L105 **Other:** LS2, PUT1, CT1, CT2, TDA1, CT3, BT1, CT4, CT5, CT6, CT7, BT2, CT8, CT9, CT10, CT11, LS61, LS64, CT15, LS88, CT21, ECE

[1]Students need not use formal terms for these properties.

[2]This standard is limited to problems posed with whole numbers and having whole number answers; students should know how to perform operations in the conventional order when there are no parentheses to specify a particular order (Order of Operations).

Number and Operations in Base Ten 3.NBT

Use place value understanding and properties of operations to perform multi-digit arithmetic.[1]

1. Use place value understanding to round whole numbers to the nearest 10 or 100.	**Power Up:** PU58, PU63, PU70, PU75, PU85, PU91, PU94, PU95, PU99, PU100, PU104 **Lessons:** L15, WP15–WP19, WP22, WP24–WP29, L30, WP30–WP41, WP50, WP51, WP53, WP70, WP90, L93, WP94, L95, WP105, WP106 **Other:** LS15, CT3, PT2, BT1, CT4, CT5, CT6, CT7, TDA4, CT9, CT10, CT13, LS93, CT19, CT20, ECE
2. Fluently add and subtract within 1000 using strategies and algorithms based on place value, properties of operations, and/or the relationship between addition and subtraction.	**Power Up:** PU11–PU21, PU29, PU31–PU34, PU47, PU53, PU59, PU81, PU82 **Lessons:** L6, L7, L8, L10, L13, WP13, L14, WP14, WP15, L16, WP16–WP18, L19, WP19, WP20, Inv2, WP21, WP22, L23, WP23, L24, WP24–WP27, L28, WP28, WP29, L30, WP30–WP35, L36, WP36–WP38, L39, WP39, L40, WP40, WP41–WP55, WP59–WP63, WP67, WP68, WP70, WP73, WP75–WP78, WP80–WP85, WP89 **Other:** LS6–LS8, LS10, LS14, CT2, LS16, CT3, PT2, BT1, CT4, LS30, CT5, CT6, LS36, LS39, LS40, CT7, BT2, CT8, CT9, CT10, CT11, BT3, CT12, TDA6, CT14, CT15, CT16, CT17, CT18, CT19, BT5, CT20, CT21, ECE
3. Multiply one-digit whole numbers by multiples of 10 in the range 10–90 (e.g., 9 x 80, 5 x 60) using strategies based on place value and properties of operations.	**Power Up:** PU79, PU85, PU87, PU88, PU90, PU93, PU96, PU99, PU107 **Lessons:** L56, L78, WP78–WP86, WP88, WP90–WP94, WP97, WP99–WP101 **Other:** LS56, CT14, LS78, CT16, CT17, ECE

Number and Operations—Fractions[2] 3.NF

Develop understanding of fractions as numbers.

1. Understand a fraction 1/*b* as the quantity formed by 1 part when a whole is partitioned into *b* equal parts; understand a fraction *a*/*b* as the quantity formed by *a* parts of size 1/*b*.	**Power Up:** PU52, PU55, PU59, PU63, PU68, PU71, PU75, PU76, PU87, PU94 **Lessons:** L29, WP29, WP31, WP33, WP36, WP37, WP39, L41, WP41, L42, WP42, L43, WP43–WP45, L46, WP46, L47, WP48–WP54, WP58, WP59, WP61–WP66, WP68–WP71, WP74, WP76, WP77, WP80, WP81, WP83–WP85, WP88, WP90, WP95, WP97, WP99, WP100 **Other:** LS29, CT6, CT7, LS41, LS42, CT8, LS46, CT9, PT5, CT10, TDA5, CT11, BT3, CT12, CT13, CT15, CT17, CT18, CT20, ECE
2. Understand a fraction as a number on the number line; represent fractions on a number line diagram.	
a. Represent a fraction 1/*b* on a number line diagram by defining the interval from 0 to 1 as the whole and partitioning it into *b* equal parts. Recognize that each part has size 1/*b* and that the endpoint of the part based at 0 locates the number 1/*b* on the number line.	**Power Up:** PU59, PU83, PU95, PU100 **Lessons:** L35, L48, WP48–WP50, WP62, WP65, WP66, WP69, WP70, WP84, WP97 **Other:** CT7, BT2, CT8, CT10, CT13, CT14, CT15, BT4, CT16, ECE
b. Represent a fraction *a*/*b* on a number line diagram by marking off *a* lengths 1/*b* from 0. Recognize that the resulting interval has size *a*/*b* and that its endpoint locates the number *a*/*b* on the number line.	**Lessons:** L35, L48, WP48–WP50, WP62, WP65, WP66, WP69, WP70, WP84, WP97 **Other:** CT7, BT2, CT8, LS48, CT10, CT13, CT14, CT15, BT4, CT16, ECE

[1]A range of algorithms may be used.

[2]Grade 3 expectations in this domain are limited to fractions with denominators 2, 3, 4, 6, and 8.

Key:	**BT:** Benchmark Test	**ET:** Extension Test	**LXA:** Lesson Extension Activity	**PUT:** Power Up Test
	CA: Calculator Activity	**Inv:** Investigation	**PS:** Problem Solving	**TDA:** Test-Day Activity
	CT: Cumulative Test	**L:** Lesson	**PT:** Performance Task	**WP:** Written Practice
	ECE: End-of-Course Exam	**LS:** Learning Station	**PU:** Power Up	

© HMH Supplemental Publishers Inc.

3. Explain equivalence of fractions in special cases, and compare fractions by reasoning about their size.	
a. Understand two fractions as equivalent (equal) if they are the same size, or the same point on a number line.	**Power Up:** PU59 **Lessons:** L46, L47, WP47, L48, WP48, WP49, WP52, WP54–WP56, WP58, WP63, WP64, WP70, WP76, WP90, WP93, WP99, WP102 **Other:** LS47, CT10, CT11, CT12
b. Recognize and generate simple equivalent fractions, e.g., 1/2 = 2/4, 4/6 = 2/3). Explain why the fractions are equivalent, e.g., by using a visual fraction model.	**Power Up:** PU59 **Lessons:** L46, L47, WP47, L48, WP48, WP49, WP50, WP52, WP54–WP56, WP58, WP63, WP64, WP70, WP76, WP90, WP93, WP99, WP102 **Other:** LS47, CT10, CT11
c. Express whole numbers as fractions, and recognize fractions that are equivalent to whole numbers.	**Lessons:** L46, WP47, L48 **Other:** LS46, CT10, CT11, BT3, CT17, CT21
d. Compare two fractions with the same numerator or the same denominator by reasoning about their size. Recognize that comparisons are valid only when the two fractions refer to the same whole. Record the results of comparisons with the symbols >, =, or <, and justify the conclusions, e.g., by using a visual fraction model.	**Power Up:** PU53, PU62 **Lessons:** L43, L49, WP50, WP59, WP61, WP62, WP64–WP66, WP68, WP69, WP75, WP80, WP81, WP102 **Other:** CT9, CT13, BT4

Measurement and Data 3.MD

Solve problems involving measurement and estimation of intervals of time, liquid volumes, and masses of objects.

1. Tell and write time to the nearest minute and measure time intervals in minutes. Solve word problems involving addition and subtraction of time intervals in minutes, e.g., by representing the problem on a number line diagram.	**Power Up:** PU1–PU30, PU32–PU34, PU36, PU37, PU39–PU47, PU49–PU51, PU53–PU56, PU58, PU61, PU62, PU64, PS69, PU71, PS71, PU72, PU76–PU78, PU85, PS87, PU89, PU90, PU92, PU94, PU99, PU102, PU103, PU107 **Lessons:** L3, WP3, WP4, L5, WP5–WP9, WP11–WP13, WP15, WP16, WP18, WP19, WP21, WP22, WP30, WP32, WP34, WP37, L38, WP38, WP39, WP42, WP44, WP45, WP55, WP57, WP63, WP65, WP66, WP68, WP70–WP73, WP75, WP81, WP83, WP84 **Other:** LS3, LS5, CT1, PT1, CT2, BT1, CT6, LXA2, LS38, BT2, CT8, CT10, ET2, BT3, CT12, CT14, BT4, CT16, ECE
2. Measure and estimate liquid volumes and masses of objects using standard units of grams (g), kilograms (kg), and liters (l).[1] Add, subtract, multiply, or divide to solve one-step word problems involving masses or volumes that are given in the same units, e.g., by using drawings (such as a beaker with a measurement scale) to represent the problem.[2]	**Lessons:** *L72, L73,* WP73–WP76, *L77,* WP77, *L78,* WP79, L80, WP80, *WP81,* WP82, *WP84,* WP86, L87, L98, WP100 **Other:** LS73, LS77, LS80, CT16, LXA7, LS87, ET7, LS98

Represent and interpret data.

3. Draw a scaled picture graph and a scaled bar graph to represent a data set with several categories. Solve one- and two-step "how many more" and "how many less" problems using information presented in scaled bar graphs.	**Lessons:** Inv1, Inv3, Inv6 **Other:** Test-Taking Strategies Guide (pp 35, 36), PUT7
4. Generate measurement data by measuring lengths using rulers marked with halves and fourths of an inch. Show the data by making a line plot, where the horizontal scale is marked off in appropriate units—whole numbers, halves, or quarters.	**Lessons:** *L34, L35, L37, L52* **Other:** *LS34, LS35, LXA1, LS37, CT7, BT2, CT8,* ET1, *CT10, BT3, CT14*

[1]Excludes compound units such as cm^3 and finding the geometric volume of a container.

[2]Excludes multiplicative comparison problems (problems involving notions of "times as much").

Geometric measurement: understand concepts of area and relate area to multiplication and to addition.

5. Recognize area as an attribute of plane figures and understand concepts of area measurement.	
a. A square with side length 1 unit, called "a unit square," is said to have "one square unit" of area, and can be used to measure area.	**Power Up:** PU93, PU103, PU108 **Lessons:** L53, WP61, L62, WP62–WP65, WP67, WP68, WP72, WP77, WP78, WP79, WP80, WP81, WP82, WP83, WP85, WP87, WP88 **Other:** CT11, CT13, BT4, BT5, CT20
b. A plane figure which can be covered without gaps or overlaps by *n* unit squares is said to have an area of *n* square units.	**Power Up:** PS82, PU93, PU103, PU108 **Lessons:** L62, L63, WP64, WP73, WP79, WP85, WP91, WP92, WP104–WP106 **Other:** CT11, CT13, BT4, BT5, CT20
6. Measure areas by counting unit squares (square cm, square m, square in, square ft, and improvised units).	**Power Up:** PS54 **Lessons:** L53, WP53, WP54, WP57–WP59, WP61, L62, WP63, WP78, WP80, L106, L108 **Other:** CT11, CT13, BT4, BT5, CT20
7. Relate area to the operations of multiplication and addition.	
a. Find the area of a rectangle with whole-number side lengths by tiling it, and show that the area is the same as would be found by multiplying the side lengths.	**Lessons:** L62, WP62, L63, WP63, L64, WP64, WP80, WP99, WP104 **Other:** CT13, BT4, BT5
b. Multiply side lengths to find areas of rectangles with whole-number side lengths in the context of solving real world and mathematical problems, and represent whole-number products as rectangular areas in mathematical reasoning.	**Power Up:** PU93, PU103, PU108 **Lessons:** L62, WP62, L63, WP63, L64, WP64, WP65, WP67, WP68, WP72, WP73, WP77, L79, WP79, WP80, WP88, WP91, WP92, WP94, WP97–WP99, WP104–WP107 **Other:** LS62, LS63, CT14, TDA7, CT15, BT4, CT16, CT17, CT19, BT5, CT20, CT21, ECE
c. Use tiling to show in a concrete case that the area of a rectangle with whole-number side lengths *a* and *b* + *c* is the sum of *a* x *b* and *a* x *c*. Use area models to represent the distributive property in mathematical reasoning.	**Lessons:** *L81(TE, Alternate Method)* **Other:** LXA6, ET6
d. Recognize area as additive. Find areas of rectilinear figures by decomposing them into non-overlapping rectangles and adding the areas of the non-overlapping parts, applying this technique to solve real world problems.	**Lessons:** *L62, WP69* **Other:** TDA7, PT8

Geometric measurement: recognize perimeter as an attribute of plane figures and distinguish between linear and area measures.

8. Solve real world and mathematical problems involving perimeters of polygons, including finding the perimeter given the side lengths, finding an unknown side length, and exhibiting rectangles with the same perimeter and different areas or with the same area and different perimeters.	**Power Up:** PU67, PU69, PU73, PU78, PU84, PU88, PU93, PU98 **Lessons:** L58, L62, WP62, L63, WP63–WP65, L66, L67, WP67, WP68, WP72, WP73, WP77, L79, WP79, WP80, WP91, WP92, WP94, WP97, WP98, WP105–WP107 **Other:** LS58, BT3, LXA3, LS62, PUT12, CT12, ET3, LXA5, CT13, CT14, ET5, LS79, CT15, CT16, PUT17, CT17, CT20, ECE

Key:
- **BT:** Benchmark Test
- **CA:** Calculator Activity
- **CT:** Cumulative Test
- **ECE:** End-of-Course Exam
- **ET:** Extension Test
- **Inv:** Investigation
- **L:** Lesson
- **LS:** Learning Station
- **LXA:** Lesson Extension Activity
- **PS:** Problem Solving
- **PT:** Performance Task
- **PU:** Power Up
- **PUT:** Power Up Test
- **TDA:** Test-Day Activity
- **WP:** Written Practice

Geometry 3.G

Reason with shapes and their attributes.

1. Understand that shapes in different categories (e.g., rhombuses, rectangles, and others) may share attributes (e.g., having four sides), and that the shared attributes can define a larger category (e.g., quadrilaterals). Recognize rhombuses, rectangles, and squares as examples of quadrilaterals, and draw examples of quadrilaterals that do not belong to any of these subcategories.	**Power Up:** PU61, PU70, PU72, PU73, PS75, PU76, PU79, PU82, PU84, PU87, PU88, PU90, PU95, PU98, PU100, PS100, PU105, PU108 **Lessons:** L51, WP51–WP60, WP64, WP65, L66, WP66, L67, WP67, WP68, L69, WP69–WP86, WP90, WP91, WP93, WP94, WP96, WP97, WP100, WP101, WP103, L104, L105, WP105–WP108, WP110 **Other:** LS51, LS52, CT11, LS66, LS67, LS69, CT14, CT15, TDA8, LXA10, LS104, CT20, ET10
2. Partition shapes into parts with equal areas. Express the area of each part as a unit fraction of the whole.	**Power Up:** PU63, PU68, PU75, PU76, PU83, PU87, PU94, PU95, PU100, PU105 **Lessons:** L42, L47, WP48, WP49, WP52, L62, WP62, L63, WP63, WP64, WP68, WP69, WP71, WP74, WP76, WP77, WP80, WP81, WP83, WP84, WP88, WP90, WP95, WP97, WP99, WP100 **Other:** LS42, CT9, CT10, LS62, LXA4, LS63, ET4

Key:

BT: Benchmark Test	**ET:** Extension Test	**LXA:** Lesson Extension Activity	**PUT:** Power Up Test
CA: Calculator Activity	**Inv:** Investigation	**PS:** Problem Solving	**TDA:** Test-Day Activity
CT: Cumulative Test	**L:** Lesson	**PT:** Performance Task	**WP:** Written Practice
ECE: End-of-Course Exam	**LS:** Learning Station	**PU:** Power Up	

LESSON
35

• Making a Line Plot to Show Measurement Data (CC.3.MD.4)

At the end of Lesson 35 complete the following activity.

Materials needed:

- ruler
- *Activity Master 1*

Vocabulary:

- **line plot:** A line plot shows information, or data, on a number line.

Measure the length of 10 crayons to the nearest fourth inch. Record the data on a line plot.

Use the number line below to make a line plot. Draw an X above the number line to show the length of each crayon. Each X stands for the length of one crayon. If two or more crayons measure the same length, stack the Xs above one another on the number line.

Lengths of Crayons (to the nearest fourth inch)

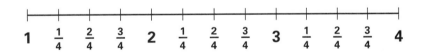

1   $\frac{1}{4}$ $\frac{2}{4}$ $\frac{3}{4}$ 2 $\frac{1}{4}$ $\frac{2}{4}$ $\frac{3}{4}$ 3 $\frac{1}{4}$ $\frac{2}{4}$ $\frac{3}{4}$ 4

Refer to the line plot to answer problems 1–3. Remember to include labels with your answers, if needed.

1. Which length was recorded the most often? _____

2. How many crayons measured more than 2 inches in length? _____

3. Count all the Xs. There are _____ in all. What does this total represent?

_____

_____

Complete *Activity Master 1.*

• Making a Line Plot to Show Measurement Data

Measure 10 items in the classroom that have a length between
3 inches and 7 inches. Measure each item to the nearest fourth inch.
Record the data on the line plot.

Lengths Measured
(to the nearest fourth inch)

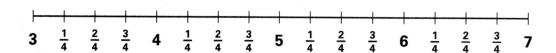

Refer to the line plot to answer problems 1–3.

1. Which length was recorded the most often?   _____

2. How many items measured less than 4 inches?   _____

3. Did more items have a length greater than or less than 5 inches?
Explain your answer.

_____

_____

• Measuring Time Intervals (CC.3.MD.1)

At the end of Lesson 38 complete the following activity.

Materials needed:

- *Activity Master 2*

We can use a diagram to help solve word problems about time.

> **Jamie rode the bus to the library. He got on the bus at 3:20 p.m. He got off the bus at 3:50 p.m. How many minutes was Jamie on the bus?**

Step 1: Use a timeline. Begin with the time Jamie got on the bus.

Step 2: Decide how you will count the minutes from 3:20 to 3:50. Draw tick marks and record the time on the timeline.

Step 3: Draw and label the jumps.

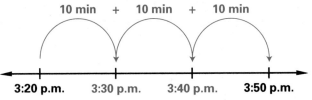

Step 4: Add to find the total minutes from 3:20 to 3:50. 10 + 10 + 10 = 30

So, Jamie was on the bus _____ minutes.

We can use a timeline and work backwards to solve word problems about time.

> **When Ray got home from the bookstore, he read his book for 25 minutes. He finished reading at 5:30 p.m. At what time did Ray start reading?**

Step 1: Use a timeline. Find Ray's finishing time on the timeline.

Step 2: Decide how you will count back 25 minutes. Draw tick marks and record the time on the timeline.

Step 3: Draw the jumps. The jumps end at _____.

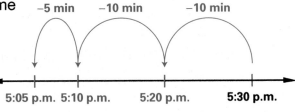

So, Ray started reading at _____.

Complete *Activity Master 2.*

Saxon Math Intermediate 3

Name _____

• Measuring Time Intervals

Use a timeline to help solve each problem.

1. Sharla's music lesson began at 4:45 p.m. and ended at 5:30 p.m. How many minutes did the music lesson last?

2. The writing contest lasted 55 minutes. It ended at 2:50 p.m. What time did the writing contest begin?

LESSON **62**

• Rectangles with the Same Area or Same Perimeter (CC.3.MD.8)

At the end of Lesson 62 complete the following activity.

Materials needed: • square tiles   • *Activity Master 3*

In Lesson 62 we measured the area and perimeter of rectangles. In this activity we will find rectangles that have the same area and compare their perimeters.

We will also find rectangles with the same perimeter and compare their areas.

Use square tiles to make two rectangles: a 2-inch by 8-inch rectangle and a 4-inch by 4-inch rectangle. Then find the area and perimeter of each rectangle.

• How are the two rectangles alike? How are they different?

_____

_____

Use tiles to make a different rectangle with the same area. Outline the rectangle on the grid.

Make as many rectangles with a perimeter of 12 inches as you can using tiles. Name each rectangle using its dimensions. Then find the area of each.

What can we conclude?

Dimensions	Area
_____ by _____	_____ square inches
_____ by _____	_____ square inches
_____ by _____	_____ square inches

_____

_____

Complete *Activity Master 3*.

• Rectangles with the Same Area or Same Perimeter

Use tiles to make as many different rectangles as possible that have an area of 12 square inches.

1. Draw the outline of each rectangle on the grid.

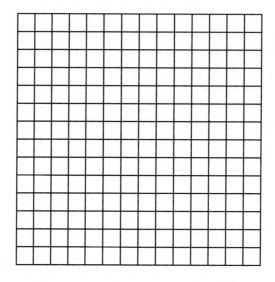

2. Write the dimensions of each rectangle and find its perimeter.

Dimensions	Perimeter
_____ by _____	_____ inches
_____ by _____	_____ inches
_____ by _____	_____ inches

3. Use the tiles to make a different rectangle that has a perimeter of 14 inches. Show the outline of the rectangle on the grid.

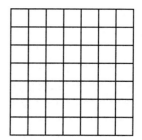

4. What is the area of the rectangle? _____

Saxon Math Intermediate 3

LESSON
63

• Relating Shapes, Fractions, and Area (CC.3.G.2)

At the end of Lesson 63 complete the following activity.

Materials needed:

• *Activity Master 4*

In Lesson 63 we used square units to describe the total area of a rectangle. In this activity we will divide rectangles into parts with equal areas and describe the area of each part using a fraction.

A rectangle is 3 yards long and 2 yards wide. Divide the rectangle into parts with equal areas. Describe the area of each part of the rectangle using a fraction.

The picture shows the area of a 3-yard by 2-yard rectangle that has been divided into equal parts.

3 yards

2 yards

The rectangle has been divided into _____ parts with equal area.

The whole rectangle has an area of _____ square yards.

The area of each part is 1 out of _____ equal parts of the total area.

1 square yard

So, the area of each part is _____ of the total area of the rectangle.

Total area is 6 square yards.

Complete *Activity Master 4.*

• Relating Shapes, Fractions, and Area

Divide each rectangle into parts with equal areas. Describe the area of each part as a fraction of the whole area of the rectangle.

1.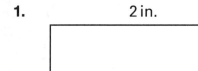

2 in.

2 in.

The area of each part is _____ of the total area of the rectangle.

2.

5 ft

2 ft

The area of each part is _____ of the total area of the rectangle.

• Finding an Unknown Side Length (CC.3.MD.8)

At the end of Lesson 67 complete the following activity.

Materials needed:

- *Activity Master 5*

Find the unknown side length, *n*.

Perimeter = 23 centimeters

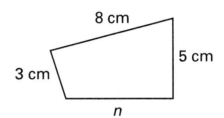

Step 1: To find the perimeter of a quadrilateral we add the lengths of all four sides.

$8 +$ _____ $+$ _____ $+ n = 23$ centimeters

Step 2: Add the known side lengths.

$16 + n = 23$

Step 3: Subtract to find the unknown side length.

$23 - 16 =$ _____

$n =$ _____ centimeters

So, the unknown side length is _____ centimeters.

Solve the problem to find the unknown side length.

Karen drew a square that has a perimeter of 20 inches. What is the length of each side of Karen's square?

We know all four sides of a square have the same length.

_____ $+$ _____ $+$ _____ $+$ _____ $= 20$ or $4 \times s = 20$

$4 \times 5 = 20$

So, each side of Karen's square has a length of _____ inches.

Complete *Activity Master 5.*

Name _____

• Finding an Unknown Side Length

Find the unknown side length.

1. Perimeter = 28 meters

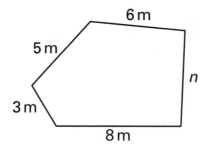

$n =$ _____ meters

2. Sal built a flower garden that is in the shape of a triangle. All three sides of the garden have the same length. The perimeter of the garden is 27 feet. What is the length of each side of the garden?

LESSON

84

• Finding Area of Combined Rectangles (CC.3.MD.7c)

At the end of Lesson 84 complete the following activity.

Materials needed:

- square tiles
- *Activity Master 6*

Vocabulary

- **Distributive Property:** A number times the sum of two addends is equal to the sum of the same number times each individual addend.

A rectangle has a width of 3 feet and a length of 14 feet. Find the area of the rectangle.

We can use square tiles to make an area model of the rectangle. Then break the model into smaller rectangles and combine the areas of the smaller rectangles to help find the answer.

Step 1: Make an area model to show 3 rows of 14.

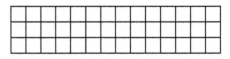

3 rows of 14 or 3 × 14

Step 2: Break apart the area model to make two smaller models for products we know.

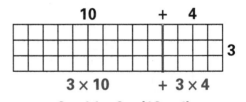

Step 3: Write the multiplication sentences for the new models. The parentheses show us which operation to do first. Multiply and then add the products to find the answer.

$3 \times 14 = 3 \times (10 + 4)$
$3 \times 14 = (3 \times 10) + (3 \times 4)$
$3 \times 14 = \quad 30 \quad + \quad 12$
$3 \times 14 = \quad\quad 42$

So, the area of the rectangle is _____ square feet.

Complete *Activity Master 6.*

• Finding Area of Combined Rectangles

Use an area model. Break the model into smaller rectangles to help solve the problem.

1. Kaylen used one-foot square tiles to make a rectangle. The rectangle is 23 feet long and 4 feet wide. What is the area of the rectangle?

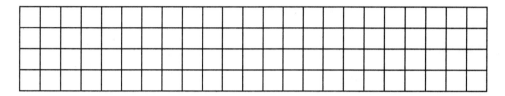

2. A rectangle has a width of 7 centimeters and a length of 13 centimeters. What is the area of the rectangle?

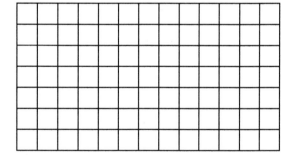

LESSON
87

• **Estimating and Measuring Liquid Volume** (CC.3.MD.2)

At the end of Lesson 87 complete the following activity.

Activity

Materials needed:

- 1-liter beaker
- *Activity Master 7*

Liquid volume can be measured using metric units such as a liter (L). Look at the 1-liter beaker and find the 1 L mark. To measure 1 liter with this beaker, we line up the top of the liquid with the 1 L mark.

Estimate how much each container will hold.

Write *more than 1 liter, about 1 liter,* or *less than 1 liter*.

1. mug   **2.** sports drink bottle   **3.** bucket

_____   _____   _____

_____   _____   _____

Complete the chart. List 3 different containers that you think would hold *more than 1 liter, about 1 liter,* or *less than 1 liter*.

More than 1 liter	About 1 liter	Less than 1 liter

Compare, analyze, and evaluate your chart and other students' charts.

Complete *Activity Master 7.*

Name ______________________________

For use with ***Lesson 87 Extension Activity***

• Estimating and Measuring Liquid Volume

Materials needed:

- 1-liter beaker, 5 different containers (labeled *A* through *E*), water

1. Estimate how many liters each container will hold. Fill in the chart below showing your estimate.

2. List the containers in order beginning with the container you think will hold the least water and ending with the one you think will hold the most water.

________________ (least)
____
____
____
________________ (most)

3. Use the beaker to measure 1 liter of water. Pour 1 liter of water into a container. Repeat until the container is full. Record the number of liters it took to fill the container. Repeat the process for each container.

Container	Estimated Number of Liters	Actual Number of Liters

4. Did you list the containers in order from the least to greatest liquid volume? If not, explain why the order should be different.

____

____

5. Audrey poured 2 liters of water into a container that holds 5 liters when full. How many more liters would it take to fill the container? Draw a picture to explain your answer.

• Using Order of Operations (CC.3.OA.8)

At the end of Lesson 92 complete the following activity.

Materials needed:

- *Activity Master 8*

Some problems with more than one operation do not have parentheses to show which operation to do first. A special set of rules, called the **order of operations**, gives the order in which calculations are done in a problem when there are no parentheses.

First, multiply and divide from left to right.

Next, add and subtract from left to right.

Use the order of operations to solve the problem below.

$30 - 4 \times 5 = x$

Step 1: Multiply from left to right.

$$30 - 4 \times 5 = x$$
$$30 - \mathbf{20} = x$$

Step 2: Subtract from left to right.

$$30 - 20 = x$$
$$\mathbf{10} = x$$

List the order of operations for each number sentence. Then follow the order of operations to solve the problem.

1. $4 + 3 \times 6 = g$

_____   _____

_____   _____

2. $8 \div 4 \times 9 = n$

_____   _____

_____   _____

Complete *Activity Master 8.*

• **Using Order of Operations**

Use the order of operations to find the unknown number.

1. $20 + 15 - 5 = h$

3. $24 - 32 \div 8 = t$

2. $36 \div 6 - 5 = d$

4. $7 \times 5 + 2 = p$

• Solving Two-Step Word Problems (CC.3.OA.8)

At the end of Lesson 95 complete the following activity.

Materials needed:

• *Activity Master 9*

We can write one equation to solve a two-step problem. Then follow the order of operations to solve the problem.

> Madison bought 3 packages of pencils. Each package has 12 pencils. Madison gave 6 pencils to her sister. How many pencils does Madison have left?

We can write $3 \times 12 - 6 = n$ to show how to solve the problem. Then we can use the order of operations to find n.

Step 1: Multiply from left to right.

$$3 \times 12 - 6 = n$$
$$36 \ - 6 = n$$

Step 2: Subtract from left to right.

$$36 - 6 = n$$
$$30 \ = n$$

So, Madison has _____ pencils left.

Explain how you know your answer is reasonable.

_____

_____

Write a word problem that can be solved using $20 - 2 \times 4$.

_____

_____

_____

Complete *Activity Master 9.*

© HMH Supplemental Publishers Inc.

Name _____

• Solving Two-Step Word Problems

Write one equation to solve each two-step problem. Then use the
order of operations to solve the problem.

1. The restaurant has 31 tables. Each table can seat 6 people. If all but
   3 seats were taken, how many people were seated at the tables?
   Explain how you know your answer is reasonable.

2. Daniel has 2 bags of balloons. Each bag has 24 balloons. He wants
   to share the balloons with 5 friends. How many balloons should
   Daniel and his friends each have? Explain how you know your answer
   is reasonable.

Saxon Math Intermediate 3

• Classifying Quadrilaterals (CC.3.G.1)

At the end of Lesson 104 complete the following activity.

Materials needed:

• *Activity Master 10*

Vocabulary:

• **rhombus:** a parallelogram with all four sides of equal length

Recall from Lesson 67 that a quadrilateral is a polygon with four sides. In this activity we will practice recognizing and classifying different types of quadrilaterals such as rhombuses, rectangles, and squares.

We can use math words to classify quadrilaterals. Describe each quadrilateral as a *parallelogram, rhombus, rectangle,* or *square*. More than one description may used.

Use the quadrilaterals to answer problems 1–4.

1. Which of the quadrilaterals are parallelograms? _____

2. Which of the quadrilaterals are rhombuses? _____

3. Why does a square have so many names? _____

_____

_____

4. Which quadrilateral is *not* a parallelogram? _____ Explain why. _____

_____

_____

Complete *Activity Master 10.*

Name _____

• Classifying Quadrilaterals

Use the quadrilaterals to answer problems 1–3.

| A | B | C | D |

1. Which quadrilaterals are rectangles? _____

2. Which quadrilaterals are rhombuses? _____

3. Which quadrilaterals are parallelograms? _____

4. Draw an example of a quadrilateral that is *not* a parallelogram.

• Making a Line Plot to Show Measurement Data

Read the problem below.

Harper collected leaves for a project. She measured the length of each leaf to the nearest fourth inch. Harper recorded the data on a line plot.

Lengths of Leaves

(to the nearest fourth inch)

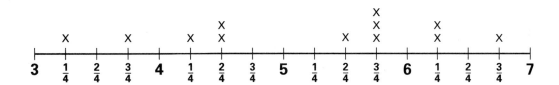

Refer to the line plot to answer the questions below. Fill in the circle with the correct answer.

1. How many leaves did Harper measure?

Ⓐ 8

Ⓑ 9

Ⓒ 10

Ⓓ 12

3. How many leaves measured less than 5 inches?

Ⓐ 4

Ⓑ 5

Ⓒ 7

Ⓓ 8

2. Which length appears the most often?

Ⓐ $3\frac{3}{4}$ inches

Ⓑ $4\frac{2}{4}$ inches

Ⓒ $5\frac{3}{4}$ inches

Ⓓ $6\frac{1}{4}$ inches

4. What was the length of the longest leaf Harper collected?

Ⓐ $3\frac{1}{4}$ inches

Ⓑ $5\frac{3}{4}$ inches

Ⓒ $6\frac{3}{4}$ inches

Ⓓ 7 inches

• Measuring Time Intervals

Use a timeline to help solve each problem. Fill in the circle with the correct answer.

1. Harry's little sister took a nap. She went to sleep at 1:30 p.m. She woke up at 2:10 p.m. How long did Harry's little sister nap?

  Ⓐ 30 minutes

  Ⓑ 35 minutes

  Ⓒ 40 minutes

  Ⓓ 45 minutes

3. It takes Margie 15 minutes to walk around the park. She finished her walk at 3:20 p.m. What time did Margie start her walk?

  Ⓐ 2:55 p.m.

  Ⓑ 3:05 p.m.

  Ⓒ 3:10 p.m.

  Ⓓ 3:30 p.m.

2. Mrs. Peno baked a cake for 50 minutes. She took the cake out of the oven at 9:45 a.m. What time did Mrs. Peno put the cake in the oven?

  Ⓐ 8:55 a.m.

  Ⓑ 9:00 a.m.

  Ⓒ 9:05 a.m.

  Ⓓ 9:10 a.m.

4. Ethan went to a ball game. The game began at 6:15 p.m. and ended at 7:10 p.m. How long did the ball game last?

  Ⓐ 30 minutes

  Ⓑ 40 minutes

  Ⓒ 50 minutes

  Ⓓ 55 minutes

• Rectangles with the Same Area or Same Perimeter

Use tiles to help solve each problem. Fill in the circle with the correct answer.

1. Which rectangle has the same area as a 4-inch by 5-inch rectangle?

    Ⓐ   3-inch by 4-inch rectangle

    Ⓑ   2-inch by 10-inch rectangle

    Ⓒ   5-inch by 5-inch rectangle

    Ⓓ   4-inch by 6-inch rectangle

2. Which rectangle has the same perimeter as a 3-inch by 3-inch rectangle?

    Ⓐ   4-inch by 4-inch rectangle

    Ⓑ   4-inch by 2-inch rectangle

    Ⓒ   5-inch by 2-inch rectangle

    Ⓓ   6-inch by 1-inch rectangle

• Relating Shapes, Fractions, and Area

Each shape is divided into parts with equal areas. Describe the area of
each part as a fraction of the whole area of the rectangle. Fill in the circle
with the correct answer.

1.

3 inches

1 inch

The area of each part is _____ of the total area of the rectangle.

Ⓐ $\frac{1}{2}$ Ⓒ $\frac{1}{4}$

Ⓑ $\frac{1}{3}$ Ⓓ $\frac{1}{6}$

2.

4 feet

2 feet

The area of each part is _____ of the total area of the rectangle.

Ⓐ $\frac{1}{5}$ Ⓒ $\frac{1}{8}$

Ⓑ $\frac{1}{6}$ Ⓓ $\frac{1}{10}$

Saxon Math Intermediate 3

• Finding an Unknown Side Length

Fill in the circle with the correct answer.

1. Find the unknown side length.

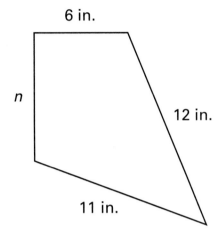

6 in.

n

12 in.

11 in.

The perimeter is 37 inches.

n = _____ inches

Ⓐ   8 inches

Ⓑ   9 inches

Ⓒ   10 inches

Ⓓ   12 inches

2. Sadie chose a tile that has six sides. All sides of the tile have the same length. The perimeter of the tile is 30 inches. What is the length of each side of the tile?

Ⓐ   3 inches

Ⓑ   4 inches

Ⓒ   5 inches

Ⓓ   8 inches

Name _____

Score _____

• Finding Area of Combined Rectangles

Draw an area model. Break the model into smaller rectangles to help solve
the problem. Fill in the circle with the correct answer.

1. Alberto used 1-centimeter square tiles to make a rectangle. The length of the
   rectangle is 16 centimeters and the width is 7 centimeters. What is the area of
   the rectangle?

   Ⓐ   23 square centimeters

   Ⓑ   46 square centimeters

   Ⓒ   112 square centimeters

   Ⓓ   122 square centimeters

2. A rectangle has a length of 15 feet and a width of 5 feet. What is the area of
   the rectangle?

   Ⓐ   75 square feet

   Ⓑ   70 square feet

   Ⓒ   65 square feet

   Ⓓ   40 square feet

• Estimating and Measuring Liquid Volume

Estimate how much each container will hold. Fill in the circle with the correct answer.

1. a fish tank

    Ⓐ less than 1 liter

    Ⓑ about 1 liter

    Ⓒ more than 1 liter

2. a juice box

    Ⓐ less than 1 liter

    Ⓑ about 1 liter

    Ⓒ more than 1 liter

Solve each word problem involving volume. You may use a drawing to represent the problem. Fill in the circle with the correct answer.

3. Keisha plans to use a 2-liter beaker to fill a container that holds 10 liters. How many 2-liter beakers will it take to fill the container?

    Ⓐ 2

    Ⓑ 4

    Ⓒ 5

    Ⓓ 6

4. Josh put 15 liters of water in a water cooler. Then he added 10 more liters. How many liters of water altogether did Josh put in the water cooler?

    Ⓐ 20 liters

    Ⓑ 25 liters

    Ⓒ 30 liters

    Ⓓ 35 liters

• Using Order of Operations

Use the order of operations to find the unknown number. Fill in the circle with the correct answer.

1. $10 + 13 - 3 = j$

   Ⓐ 20

   Ⓑ 23

   Ⓒ 26

   Ⓓ 30

3. $24 - 48 \div 8 = r$

   Ⓐ 3

   Ⓑ 16

   Ⓒ 18

   Ⓓ 20

2. $56 \div 7 - 3 = m$

   Ⓐ 14

   Ⓑ 11

   Ⓒ   5

   Ⓓ   4

4. $9 \times 5 + 5 = s$

   Ⓐ 45

   Ⓑ 50

   Ⓒ 55

   Ⓓ 90

• Solving Two-Step Word Problems

Write one equation to solve each two-step problem. Then use the order of
operations to solve the problem. Fill in the circle with the correct answer.

1. Cori and Austin plan to buy a
remote control car together that
costs $59. Each boy has $17. How
much more money do the boys
need to buy the car?

  Ⓐ $22

  Ⓑ $25

  Ⓒ $35

  Ⓓ $42

3. Roger and 4 of his friends found
20 seashells on the beach. At the
end of the day, the boys each took
an equal number of seashells.
On his way home, Roger found
3 more seashells. How many
seashells does Roger have?

  Ⓐ 23

  Ⓑ 10

  Ⓒ 8

  Ⓓ 7

2. Layla went to the bookstore.
She bought 3 books that cost $6
each and a puzzle that cost $7.
How much did Layla spend at
the bookstore?

  Ⓐ $25

  Ⓑ $27

  Ⓒ $39

  Ⓓ $45

4. During Saturday's basketball
game, Matt made 7 shots that
were worth 2 points each. He
made 1 shot that was worth
3 points. How many points did
Matt score?

  Ⓐ 12

  Ⓑ 13

  Ⓒ 17

  Ⓓ 22

• Classifying Quadrilaterals

Use the quadrilaterals to answer problems 1–3. Fill in the circle with the correct answer.

   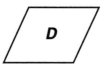

1. Which quadrilateral is a rhombus?

Ⓐ A

Ⓑ B

Ⓒ C

Ⓓ D

2. Which quadrilateral is *not* a parallelogram?

Ⓐ A

Ⓑ B

Ⓒ C

Ⓓ D

3. Which word can be used to describe all the shapes?

Ⓐ rectangle

Ⓑ parallelogram

Ⓒ rhombus

Ⓓ quadrilateral

4. A rectangle can also be classified as a _____.

Ⓐ triangle

Ⓑ rhombus

Ⓒ parallelogram

Ⓓ square

Lesson Extension Activity Answers

Lesson Extension Activity 1
See student work.
Answers 1–3 will vary.

Lesson Extension Activity 2
30
5:05 p.m.; 5:05 p.m.

Lesson Extension Activity 3
They have the same area. They have different perimeters. Grid: 1-in. by 16-in. rectangle; Chart: 3-in. by 3-in., 9 sq in.; 4-in. by 2-in., 8 sq in.; 5-in. by 1-in., 5 sq in.

Lesson Extension Activity 4
6; 6; 6; $\frac{1}{6}$

Lesson Extension Activity 5
7 centimeters; 5 inches

Lesson Extension Activity 6
42 square feet

Lesson Extension Activity 7
1. less than 1 liter
2. about 1 liter
3. more than 1 liter
Chart: Answers will vary.

Lesson Extension Activity 8
1. multiply, add; $g = 22$
2. divide, multiply; $n = 18$

Lesson Extension Activity 9
30; We can round. $3 \times 10 - 6 = 24$. Since 24 is close to 30, we know our answer is reasonable. See student work.

Lesson Extension Activity 10
1. A, B, C, and D
2. B and D
3. See student work.
4. E; It does not have 2 pair of parallel sides.

Activity Master Answers

Activity Master 1
See student work.
Answers 1–3 will vary.

Activity Master 2
1. See student work. 45 minutes
2. See student work. 1:55 p.m.

Activity Master 3
1. See student work.
2. 3-in. by 4-in., 14 in.; 2-in. by 6-in., 16 in.; 12-in. by 1-in., 26 in.
3. 2-in. by 5-in. or 1-in. by 6-in.
4. 10 sq in. or 6 sq in.

Activity Master 4
See student work.
1. $\frac{1}{4}$ 2. $\frac{1}{10}$

Activity Master 5
1. 6 meters   2. 9 feet

Activity Master 6
1. 92 square feet
2. 91 square centimeters

Activity Master 7
See student work.
Answers 1–4 will vary.
5. 3 liters

Activity Master 8
1. 30   3. 20
2. 1   4. 37

Activity Master 9
1. 183 people; See student work.
2. 8 balloons; See student work.

Activity Master 10
1. A and C
2. A and B
3. A, B, C, and D
4. See student work.

Extension Test Answers

Extension Test 1
1. Ⓓ 12
2. Ⓒ $5\frac{3}{4}$ inches
3. Ⓑ 5
4. Ⓒ $6\frac{3}{4}$ inches

Extension Test 2
1. Ⓒ 40 minutes
2. Ⓐ 8:55 a.m.
3. Ⓑ 3:05 p.m.
4. Ⓓ 55 minutes

Extension Test 3
1. Ⓑ 2-inch by 10-inch rectangle
2. Ⓑ 4-inch by 2-inch rectangle

Extension Test 4
1. Ⓑ $\frac{1}{3}$
2. Ⓒ $\frac{1}{8}$

Extension Test 5
1. Ⓐ 8 inches
2. Ⓒ 5 inches

Extension Test 6
1. Ⓒ 112 square centimeters
2. Ⓐ 75 square feet

Extension Test 7
1. Ⓒ more than 1 liter
2. Ⓐ less than 1 liter
3. Ⓒ 5
4. Ⓑ 25 liters

Extension Test 8
1. Ⓐ 20
2. Ⓒ 5
3. Ⓒ 18
4. Ⓑ 50

Extension Test 9
1. Ⓑ $25
2. Ⓐ $25
3. Ⓓ 7
4. Ⓒ 17

Extension Test 10
1. Ⓐ A
2. Ⓑ B
3. Ⓓ quadrilateral
4. Ⓒ parallelogram